Fact Finders®

The
Solar System
and Beyond

Our Moon

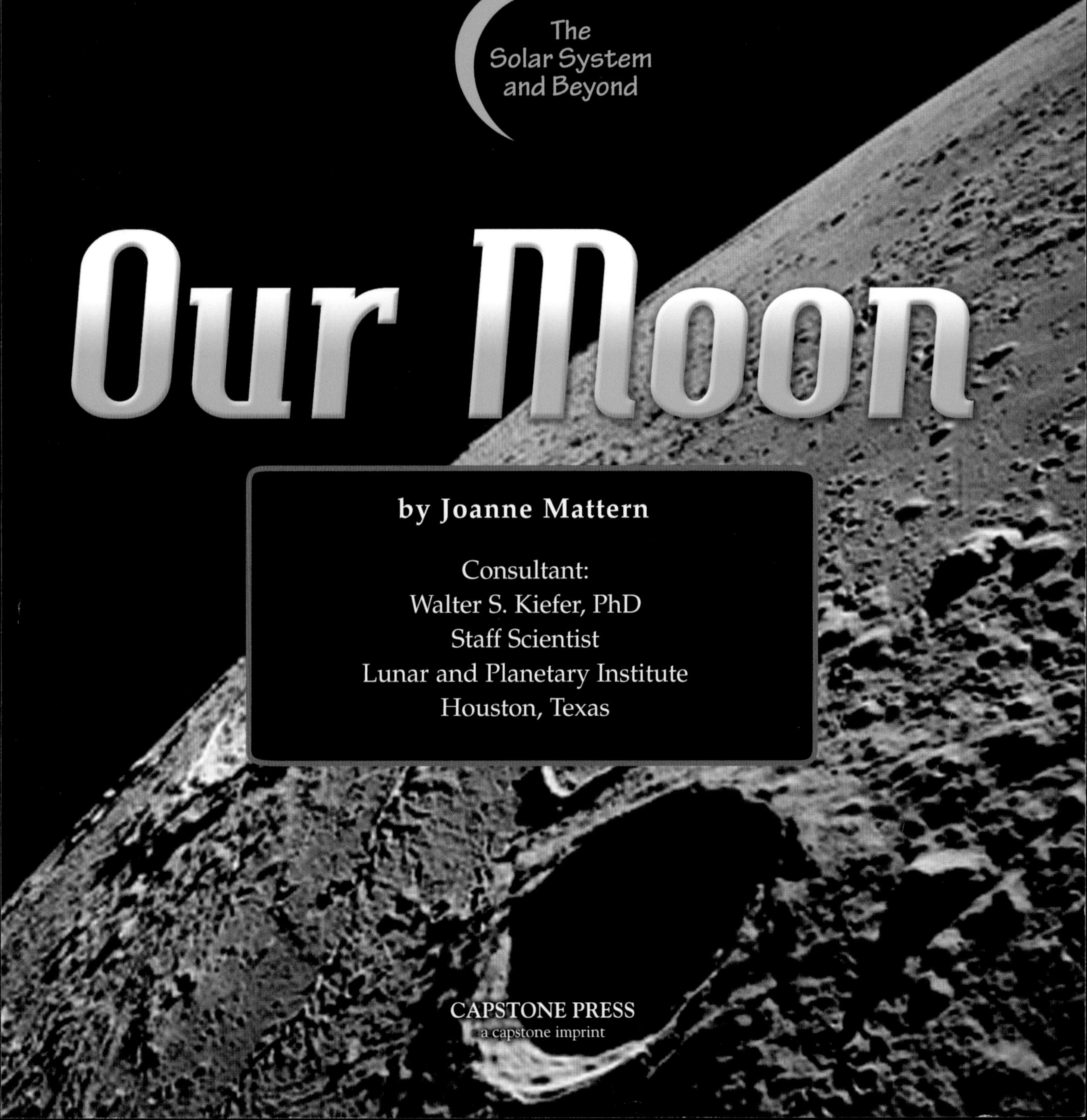

by Joanne Mattern

Consultant:
Walter S. Kiefer, PhD
Staff Scientist
Lunar and Planetary Institute
Houston, Texas

CAPSTONE PRESS
a capstone imprint

Fact Finders are published by Capstone Press,
151 Good Counsel Drive, P.O. Box 669, Mankato, Minnesota 56002.
www.capstonepub.com

 Books published by Capstone Press are manufactured with paper
containing at least 10 percent post-consumer waste.

Library of Congress Cataloging-in-Publication Data
Mattern, Joanne, 1963-
 Our moon / by Joanne Mattern.
 p. cm.—(Fact finders. The solar system and beyond)
 Includes bibliographical references and index.
 Summary: "Describes Earth's moon, including its orbit, features, and affect on
Earth"—Provided by publisher.
 ISBN 978-1-4296-5394-7 (library binding)
 ISBN 978-1-4296-6239-0 (paperback)
 1. Moon—Juvenile literature. I. Title. II. Series.
 QB582.M38 2011
 523.3—dc22   2010027377

Editorial Credits
Jennifer Besel, editor; Heidi Thompson, designer; Eric Manske, production specialist

Photo Credits
Capstone Press, 9; Comstock Images: 11(moon), 13, 25(moon); DigitalVision, 3; iStockphoto: Manfred
Konrad, 23; NASA, 17; NASA/JPL/USGS, 19; NASA/JSC scan by Kipp Teague, 1, 14, 27; NASA/
NSSDC, 15; Photo Researchers, Inc: BSIP, 21, David A. Hardy, 7; Photodisc, cover, 11(Earth), 25(Earth),
29; Shutterstock: Ioana Drutu, 5, J.K. York, 22

Artistic Effects
iStockphoto: appleuzr, Dar Yang Yan, Nickilford

Printed in the United States of America in Stevens Point, Wisconsin.
092010   005934WZS11

Table of Contents

Chapter 1

Earth's Neighbor

Look up at the sky on a clear night, and you can usually see the Moon. It's hard to miss. It is the brightest object in the night sky. The Moon is so bright because it is Earth's closest neighbor. It's about 238,855 miles (384,400 kilometers) away.

Even though the Moon and Earth are close neighbors, they are very different places. Earth is full of life. It has oceans and continents. It supports billions of plants, animals, and people. The Moon has no life at all. It is a dry rock without any weather.

Because the Moon is close to Earth, scientists have learned a lot about it. Twelve people have even walked on the Moon. They helped us discover what the Moon is like and how it affects us here on Earth.

What Is a Moon?

Earth isn't the only planet that has a moon. In fact, most planets and dwarf planets have moons. But what is a moon? A moon is an object that **orbits** a planet or dwarf planet instead of the Sun.

Scientists divide moons into two groups—regular and irregular. Regular moons are large and have unchanging orbits. Earth's moon fits into this group. Irregular moons are small and orbit far away from a planet. Their orbits also tilt and change.

Scientists think regular moons formed in one of two ways. Some regular moons formed from the same gases and dust that created the planet they orbit. Others were created by an object hitting a planet. Earth's Moon might have been formed by such a crash. Scientists believe about 4.6 billion years ago a Mars-sized object smashed into Earth. The crash caused a cloud of material to break away. Over time, the cloud cooled and shrank into the Moon.

Scientists aren't sure how irregular moons form. Some think these moons are asteroids or comets that were captured by a planet's **gravity**.

orbit: the path an object follows as it goes around a planet

gravity: a force that pulls objects together

Planets' Moons

Planet	Number of Moons
Mercury	0
Venus	0
Earth	1
Mars	2
Jupiter	more than 60
Saturn	more than 60
Uranus	27
Neptune	13

illustration of how Earth's Moon might have formed

Circling Earth

The Moon goes about 2,288 miles (3,682 km) per hour as it travels around Earth. At that speed it takes about 708 hours for the Moon to circle Earth once. We call that time a **lunar** month.

But what keeps the moon circling Earth? Two forces keep the moon in place. Earth's gravity pulls the Moon toward the planet. This constant tugging is called centripetal (sen-TRIP-uh-tuhl) force. At the same time, centrifugal (sen-TRIF-uh-guhl) force is also working on the Moon. Centrifugal force causes objects to move outward as they spin. Think of how you feel on a spinning carnival ride. Centrifugal force pushes you back against your seat as the ride whirls around. The forces that pull and push on the Moon are equal. That balance keeps the Moon orbiting Earth.

lunar: to do with the Moon

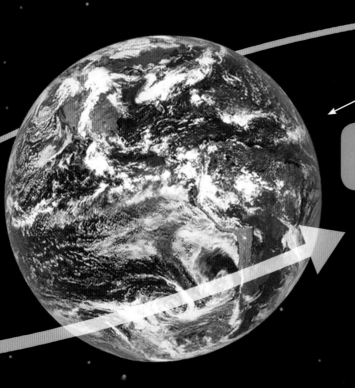

centrifugal force pushes the Moon away from Earth

centripetal force pulls the Moon toward Earth

Spinning Around

The Moon also rotates around its own **axis**. All planets, dwarf planets, and moons spin like tops. Earth rotates in 24 hours. We call that a day. It takes the Moon 708 hours, or 29.5 Earth-days, to rotate once. That means a lunar day is the same length as a lunar month.

Did you know the same side of the Moon always faces Earth? It's true! From Earth, we can't see the far side of the Moon. The Moon's rotation and orbit are the same length. That means the Moon spins at the same speed that it circles Earth. So the same side always faces our planet.

FACT: People saw the far side of the Moon for the first time in 1959. A spacecraft called *Luna 3* took pictures of this never-seen side of the Moon.

axis: an imaginary line that runs through the middle of a moon

The Moon's Rotation

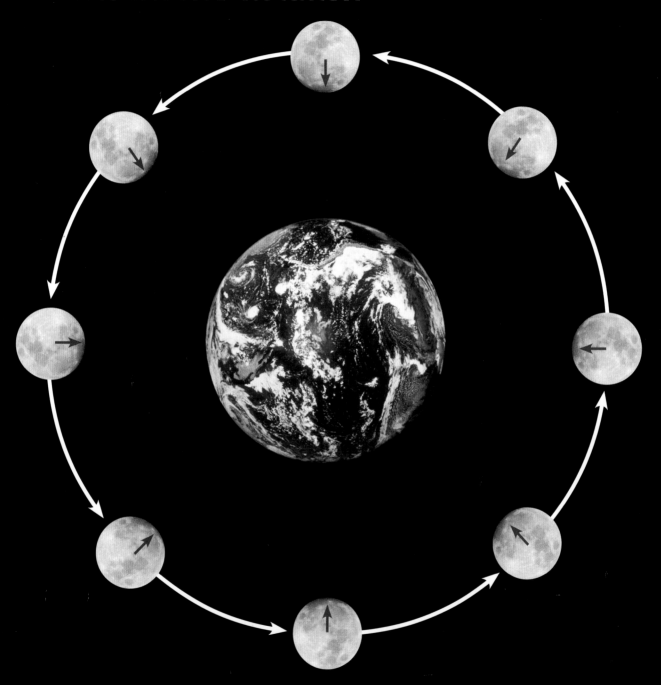

* red arrow shows how the same side
of the Moon always faces Earth

Chapter 2

On The Moon

The Moon is about 6,783 miles (10,916 km) around. How long would it take to drive around the Moon? Going 60 miles (97 km) per hour, it would take just over 113 hours.

Earth's Moon isn't the biggest moon in the solar system. The largest moon is Ganymede, one of Jupiter's moons. Ganymede has a **diameter** of 3,282 miles (5,282 km).

Our Moon might not be the largest in the solar system. But it is one of the largest compared to the size of the planet it orbits. Most moons are much smaller than their planet. But in space terms, the Moon and Earth are fairly close in size.

diameter: a straight line through the center of a planet, from one side to the other

A Little Gravity

Even though they are close in size, the Moon is less **dense** than Earth. And the less dense something is, the weaker its gravity. In fact, the Moon's gravity is about six times weaker than Earth's. That means things aren't as heavy on the Moon as they are on Earth. If you weigh 90 pounds (41 kilograms) here, you would weigh only 15 pounds (7 kg) on the Moon!

dense: thick or crowded

the Moon compared to Earth

Coming to the Surface

Earth's surface has lots of color—green grass, brown dirt, blue water. The Moon's surface is very different. The Moon is covered with dark gray dust called regolith. Regolith is made of crushed bits of rock. The Moon is all gray, all the time.

The Moon has many holes, or craters, in its gray surface. There are millions of craters on the Moon. Some craters are so large, there are mountains in the middle of them!

All those craters show that the Moon had a violent past. Over billions of years, asteroids and comets struck the Moon. They still do today, though not as often. These crashes formed craters in the Moon's surface.

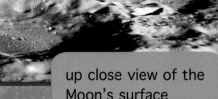

up close view of the Moon's surface

FACT: The Moon does not produce its own light. Moonlight is actually the Moon reflecting sunlight back to Earth.

From Earth, some parts of the Moon's surface look light, while others are dark. The lighter areas are mountains called highlands. The highlands are generally the highest locations on the Moon. In fact, some Moon mountains are more than 4 miles (6 km) high.

The dark areas on the Moon are called maria. Maria is the Latin word for "seas." Scientists chose this name because the dark areas look like large bodies of water. But maria are not lakes. They are huge plains of hardened lava.

It might be hard to believe, but there were volcanoes on the Moon billions of years ago. Moon volcanoes were small domes only a few hundred feet high. But scientists don't expect any more eruptions on the Moon. It's been at least a billion years since any of these volcanoes erupted.

Maria make up more than 16 percent of the Moon's surface. These dark areas are covered with craters. They also have long channels called rilles. The rilles were probably formed when hot lava from volcanoes flowed across the surface. Rilles are so large they can be seen from Earth with a small telescope.

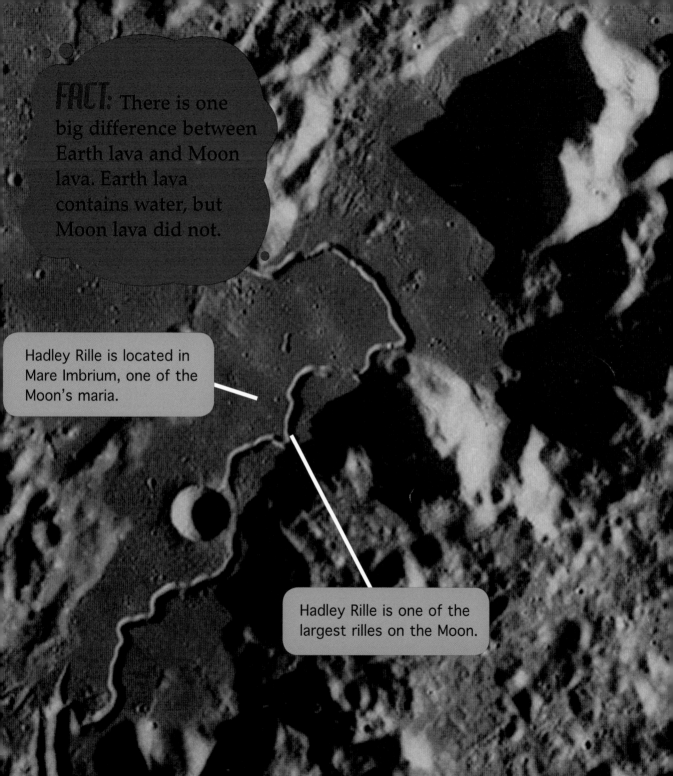

FACT: There is one big difference between Earth lava and Moon lava. Earth lava contains water, but Moon lava did not.

Hadley Rille is located in Mare Imbrium, one of the Moon's maria.

Hadley Rille is one of the largest rilles on the Moon.

Nothing Like Earth

The surface of the Moon is nothing like Earth's surface. The Moon has no life. It also has no **atmosphere**. The Moon's gravity is too weak to hold on to gases. Because there is no atmosphere, the Moon's sky is always black. The stars can always be seen. Earth's atmosphere makes stars look like they twinkle. Without an atmosphere, stars don't twinkle on the Moon.

Not having an atmosphere affects more than just how the sky looks. Without an atmosphere, wind doesn't form on the Moon. There is also no liquid water on the surface. No wind or water means there is no weather on the Moon. There's no breeze to ruffle your hair and no rain to wet the ground. The Moon is totally quiet too. There is no air to carry noise from place to place.

atmosphere: the layer of gases that surrounds some moons and planets

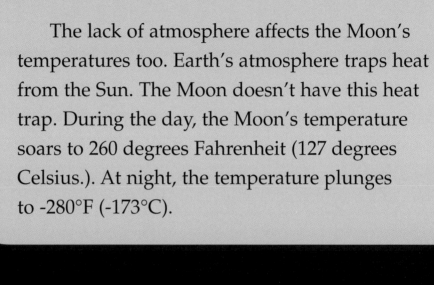

The lack of atmosphere affects the Moon's temperatures too. Earth's atmosphere traps heat from the Sun. The Moon doesn't have this heat trap. During the day, the Moon's temperature soars to 260 degrees Fahrenheit (127 degrees Celsius.). At night, the temperature plunges to -280°F (-173°C).

the sky from the Moon's surface

Chapter 3

The Moon from Earth

The Moon does not look the same in Earth's sky every night. It looks like it changes shape. These different shapes are called phases. During these phases, the Moon doesn't actually change. Our view changes as the Moon orbits Earth.

During its orbit, the Moon comes between Earth and the Sun. In this phase, the side of the Moon near Earth faces away from the Sun. It can't reflect sunlight. This phase is called the new moon. We can't see the Moon during this phase.

As it continues its orbit, more of the Moon's near side faces the Sun. Each night the Moon reflects more sunlight and looks bigger. Finally, the Moon arrives at a place directly facing the Sun. Sunlight shines on all of the near side of the Moon. This light creates the bright full moon. After the full moon, the Moon continues around Earth. It appears to get smaller and smaller. Finally, it reaches the new moon phase again, and the cycle starts over.

Phases of the Moon

sunlight

last crescent

last quarter

gibbous

new moon

full moon

sunlight

first crescent

first quarter

gibbous

Eclipses

The Sun, Moon, and Earth line up differently as they move through space. Sometimes Earth lines up exactly between the Sun and the full Moon. Then Earth casts a shadow on the Moon. This shadow changes the Moon's bright white color to a reddish brown. This event is called a lunar eclipse. Lunar eclipses can happen up to three times a year.

eclipse: an event in which Earth's shadow passes over the Moon or the Moon's shadow passes over Earth

lunar eclipse

solar eclipse

Once in a while, a new moon lines up exactly between the Sun and Earth. The Moon blocks out the Sun's light and shadows Earth. The sky turns dark, and stars can be seen during the day. This event is called a solar eclipse. Solar eclipses are rare. Only one or two happen on Earth each year. And they can only be seen by people who are directly facing the path of the eclipse. Any location on Earth will only see a total solar eclipse about once every 360 years.

Changing Tides

Earth's gravity keeps the Moon nearby. But the Moon's gravity affects Earth too. The Moon's gravity changes the **tides** in Earth's large bodies of water. During high tides, waves move higher up the beach or coastline. In low tides, waves crash farther away from the coastline.

So how does the Moon change sea levels? As Earth rotates, bodies of water take turns facing the Moon. When a body of water faces the Moon, the Moon's gravity pulls on the water. The water has high tide. Bodies of water that face directly away from the Moon experience high tide at the same time. Waters that are not directly facing toward or away from the Moon have low tide. When the Earth turns, the Moon's gravity pulls on other bodies of water, and the tides change.

tide: the constant change in sea level

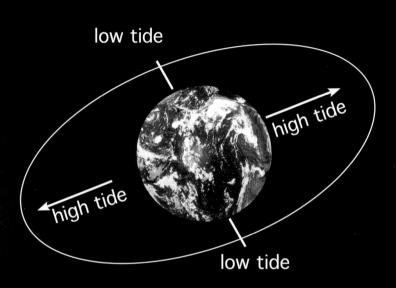

low tide

high tide

high tide

low tide

FACT: The biggest tide change happens in Canada's Bay of Fundy. The difference between high and low tides is sometimes more than 50 feet (15 m).

Chapter 4

Exploring the Moon

People have studied the Moon for thousands of years. Early astronomers looked through simple telescopes. Today scientists can hold actual rocks from Earth's nearest neighbor.

In January 1959, the Soviet Union's *Luna 1* was the first spacecraft to fly past the Moon. Two months later, the United States sent *Pioneer 4* past the Moon. These spacecraft and the ones that followed took photos of the Moon.

Then on July 20, 1969, U.S. astronauts Neil Armstrong and Buzz Aldrin became the first people to walk on the Moon. These astronauts conducted experiments and made observations. They brought back rocks for scientists to study. Their experiments helped scientists learn what the Moon was made of and how it formed. Between 1969 and 1972, five more missions landed astronauts on the Moon.

FACT: Since there is no weather on the Moon, the surface changes very slowly. That is why the footprints left by astronauts more than 40 years ago are still there today.

No one has stepped foot on the Moon in almost 40 years. But we're still exploring it. Several spacecraft orbited the Moon during the 1990s, taking photographs and making maps. In 1998, a **probe** called *Lunar Prospector* orbited the Moon and studied its magnetic fields and chemicals. In June 2009, the United States launched the *Lunar Reconnaissance Orbiter*, which is still making observations. Other nations, including China and the European Union, have also sent spacecraft to the Moon.

In September 2009, one of the most startling Moon discoveries occurred. Three probes discovered evidence of water under the Moon's surface. This discovery shattered the idea that the Moon was totally dry and dead.

probe: a small vehicle used to explore objects in space

No one knows how our future will be tied to the Moon. Perhaps one day astronauts will use the Moon as a stopover for trips to Mars. Or maybe people will someday live on the Moon. For now, Earth's closest neighbor will continue to light our nights.

Glossary

atmosphere (AT-muh-sfeer)—the layer of gases that surrounds some dwarf planets, planets, moons, and stars

axis (AK-sis)—an imaginary line that runs through the middle of a dwarf planet, moon, or planet; a dwarf planet, moon, or planet spins on its axis

dense (DENSS)—thick or crowded

diameter (dye-AM-uh-tur)—a straight line through the center of a circle, from one side to the other

eclipse (i-KLIPS)—an astronomical event in which Earth's shadow passes over the Moon or the Moon's shadow passes over Earth

gravity (GRAV-uh-tee)—a force that pulls objects together; gravity increases as the mass of objects increases or as objects get closer

lunar (LOO-nur)—to do with the Moon

orbit (OR-bit)—the path an object follows as it goes around a dwarf planet, planet, or star

probe (PROHB)—a small vehicle used to explore objects in outer space

tide (TIDE)—the constant change in sea level that is caused by the pull of the Moon on Earth

Read More

Allyn, Daisy. *The Moon: Earth's Satellite*. Our Solar System. New York: Gareth Stevens Pub., 2011.

Carson, Mary Kay. *Far-Out Guide to the Moon*. Far-Out Guide to the Solar System. Berkeley Heights, N.J.: Enslow Publishers, 2011.

Hicks, Terry Allan. *Earth and the Moon*. Space! New York: Marshall Cavendish Benchmark, 2010.

Kortenkamp, Steve. *The Planets of Our Solar System*. The Solar System and Beyond. Mankato, Minn.: Capstone Press, 2011.

Internet Sites

FactHound offers a safe, fun way to find Internet sites related to this book. All of the sites on FactHound have been researched by our staff.

Here's all you do:

Visit *www.facthound.com*

Type in this code: 9781429653947

 Check out projects, games and lots more at
www.capstonekids.com

Index